A short history of Barbados, from its first discovery and settlement to the present time. A new edition, corrected and enlarged.

George. Frere

A short history of Barbados, from its first discovery and settlement to the present time. A new edition, corrected and enlarged.
Frere, George.
ESTCID: T092935
Reproduction from British Library
Anonymous. By George Frere. With a half-title.
London : printed for J. Dodsley, 1768.
[2],xiii,[1],132p. ; 8°

Eighteenth Century
Collections Online
Print Editions

Gale ECCO Print Editions

Relive history with *Eighteenth Century Collections Online*, now available in print for the independent historian and collector. This series includes the most significant English-language and foreign-language works printed in Great Britain during the eighteenth century, and is organized in seven different subject areas including literature and language; medicine, science, and technology; and religion and philosophy. The collection also includes thousands of important works from the Americas.

The eighteenth century has been called "The Age of Enlightenment." It was a period of rapid advance in print culture and publishing, in world exploration, and in the rapid growth of science and technology – all of which had a profound impact on the political and cultural landscape. At the end of the century the American Revolution, French Revolution and Industrial Revolution, perhaps three of the most significant events in modern history, set in motion developments that eventually dominated world political, economic, and social life.

In a groundbreaking effort, Gale initiated a revolution of its own: digitization of epic proportions to preserve these invaluable works in the largest online archive of its kind. Contributions from major world libraries constitute over 175,000 original printed works. Scanned images of the actual pages, rather than transcriptions, recreate the works *as they first appeared.*

Now for the first time, these high-quality digital scans of original works are available via print-on-demand, making them readily accessible to libraries, students, independent scholars, and readers of all ages.

For our initial release we have created seven robust collections to form one the world's most comprehensive catalogs of 18th century works.

Initial Gale ECCO Print Editions collections include:

History and Geography
Rich in titles on English life and social history, this collection spans the world as it was known to eighteenth-century historians and explorers. Titles include a wealth of travel accounts and diaries, histories of nations from throughout the world, and maps and charts of a world that was still being discovered. Students of the War of American Independence will find fascinating accounts from the British side of conflict.

Social Science
Delve into what it was like to live during the eighteenth century by reading the first-hand accounts of everyday people, including city dwellers and farmers, businessmen and bankers, artisans and merchants, artists and their patrons, politicians and their constituents. Original texts make the American, French, and Industrial revolutions vividly contemporary.

Medicine, Science and Technology
Medical theory and practice of the 1700s developed rapidly, as is evidenced by the extensive collection, which includes descriptions of diseases, their conditions, and treatments. Books on science and technology, agriculture, military technology, natural philosophy, even cookbooks, are all contained here.

Literature and Language
Western literary study flows out of eighteenth-century works by Alexander Pope, Daniel Defoe, Henry Fielding, Frances Burney, Denis Diderot, Johann Gottfried Herder, Johann Wolfgang von Goethe, and others. Experience the birth of the modern novel, or compare the development of language using dictionaries and grammar discourses.

Religion and Philosophy
The Age of Enlightenment profoundly enriched religious and philosophical understanding and continues to influence present-day thinking. Works collected here include masterpieces by David Hume, Immanuel Kant, and Jean-Jacques Rousseau, as well as religious sermons and moral debates on the issues of the day, such as the slave trade. The Age of Reason saw conflict between Protestantism and Catholicism transformed into one between faith and logic -- a debate that continues in the twenty-first century.

Law and Reference
This collection reveals the history of English common law and Empire law in a vastly changing world of British expansion. Dominating the legal field is the *Commentaries of the Law of England* by Sir William Blackstone, which first appeared in 1765. Reference works such as almanacs and catalogues continue to educate us by revealing the day-to-day workings of society.

Fine Arts
The eighteenth-century fascination with Greek and Roman antiquity followed the systematic excavation of the ruins at Pompeii and Herculaneum in southern Italy; and after 1750 a neoclassical style dominated all artistic fields. The titles here trace developments in mostly English-language works on painting, sculpture, architecture, music, theater, and other disciplines. Instructional works on musical instruments, catalogs of art objects, comic operas, and more are also included.

The BiblioLife Network

This project was made possible in part by the BiblioLife Network (BLN), a project aimed at addressing some of the huge challenges facing book preservationists around the world. The BLN includes libraries, library networks, archives, subject matter experts, online communities and library service providers. We believe every book ever published should be available as a high-quality print reproduction; printed on-demand anywhere in the world. This insures the ongoing accessibility of the content and helps generate sustainable revenue for the libraries and organizations that work to preserve these important materials.

The following book is in the "public domain" and represents an authentic reproduction of the text as printed by the original publisher. While we have attempted to accurately maintain the integrity of the original work, there are sometimes problems with the original work or the micro-film from which the books were digitized. This can result in minor errors in reproduction. Possible imperfections include missing and blurred pages, poor pictures, markings and other reproduction issues beyond our control. Because this work is culturally important, we have made it available as part of our commitment to protecting, preserving, and promoting the world's literature.

GUIDE TO FOLD-OUTS MAPS and OVERSIZED IMAGES

The book you are reading was digitized from microfilm captured over the past thirty to forty years. Years after the creation of the original microfilm, the book was converted to digital files and made available in an online database.

In an online database, page images do not need to conform to the size restrictions found in a printed book. When converting these images back into a printed bound book, the page sizes are standardized in ways that maintain the detail of the original. For large images, such as fold-out maps, the original page image is split into two or more pages

Guidelines used to determine how to split the page image follows:

- Some images are split vertically; large images require vertical and horizontal splits.
- For horizontal splits, the content is split left to right.
- For vertical splits, the content is split from top to bottom.
- For both vertical and horizontal splits, the image is processed from top left to bottom right.

A SHORT HISTORY

OF

BARBADOS.

A

SHORT HISTORY

OF

BARBADOS,

FROM

Its First Discovery and Settlement

TO

The Present Time.

A NEW EDITION,
Corrected and Enlarged.

LONDON,
Printed for J. DODSLEY, in Pall-Mall.
MDCCLXVIII.

PREFACE.

THE Author of the following sheets hath endeavoured faithfully, and impartially, to relate the events that concern the ancient colony of Barbados. His motive to this attempt, was in some degree a gratification of his amusement, by filling up some leisure hours, in a manner not totally useless to himself or the public;

public; but principally to shew, that Barbados hath always preserved a uniform and steady attachment to Great Britain, and therefore is intitled to the affection and indulgence of the mother country. All people naturally wish to receive some account of their native country; of its constitution, and its progress to power and opulence. If then this short performance, meets the approbation, or adds to the amusement, or gratifies the curiosity, of the natives of that island, the Author will think the time he has employed in this composition not misspent.

He

He is aware, that some readers will think this volume too concise; in truth, he intended it only as an introduction to a more general history; but he has neither inclination or phlegm enough to spin out so dry a subject to a greater length: some one with equal leisure, and greater abilities, may improve, and make more perfect, this work. He knows that there may be other readers who will attempt to discover greater faults; these should read the fable of the Miller, his Son, and their Ass. To satisfy the generality of the world, is highly improbable; to please the whole of it, impossible: we continually find that very able authors, writing upon the most important subjects, are roughly handled by the artful critic; how then can a writer expect to escape, who wishes not for applause, but is ambitious only of serving the country he treats of, and who cares not a jot for the censorious critic's rod.—What is said upon the subject of Privileges, is offered only for the benefit of Barbados, and for no other view or reason whatever: As to the supposition of this part of the history being intended to injure any man, 'tis a thought the Author despises, as heartily as he does the remark-

remarker who suggested it: the Hero of the page must be represented in his true colours, which are really not intended (nor never were intended) to be exaggerated; though the Author must confess, he is not sorry, if the lot has fallen to a Don-Quixot-like Knight.

Indeed it is strange, that not any a Historical Account hath ever ap-

[a] Ligon's Account does not contain a space of forty years, and only tells us of the first settlers. The Account of Barbados in the British Empire in America is a very small part of a large work in two volumes. Whether the Memoirs of the first Settlement of Barbados, published in 1742, can be called an Historical Account, must be submitted to the Reader.

peared of an island of so much consequence to the mother country as Barbados is, whose loyalty has often been experienced; whose assistance never was denied; and whose acquiescence to the authority of Great Britain [b] a late remarkable instance has fully exemplified. An island too, to which belongs a merit peculiar to itself; it has not, for threescore years past, cost one shilling of expence to Great Britain, except a few pieces of cannon that were granted upon application many years ago; what salaries are paid by the crown to its

[b] Stamp Act.

officers,

officers, are all provided by the four and half *per cent.* duty.

The distance of time and place, and the difficulty of gathering materials, will, it is hoped, excuse any misrepresentations, or other errors that may appear in this work. The Author's acquaintance with many of the circumstances he relates, authentic matters of record, and the assistance of some old writers, as well as some of modern date, have enabled him to throw together the following anecdotes. He hath been particularly attentive to the relation of facts. Truth ought to be the foundation upon which every

scrib-

[x]

scribbling builder should erect his fabric; notwithstanding the pleasant remark of an ingenious [c] author, whose works the actions of mankind give too great sanction to. "Truth," says this elegant writer, "by her native beauty is "sure to charm; yet, from her re- "pugnancy to most men's interests, "she is seldom welcome; politici- "ans are afraid of her, parties de- "test her, and all professions agree, "that she is very dangerous if suf- "fered to go about in public."

[c] Jenyns's Origin of Evil.

WHEN this edition was preparing for the press, the Author was favored with a sight of some remarks, published in Barbados, upon the first edition of this work. These remarks contain some assertions that are false, many confutable, and all of them uncandid, and ungenerous. They are written with the peevishness of a child, whose play-things have been disturbed; and with an impetuosity, that shews the remarker has been touched upon a sore part, and that he has felt the rub. The remarker will not be indulged with a reply, because a reply would be food for his distempered appetite, and would run him into his delightful, hobby-horsical labyrinth, through which Job's patience only could support the pursuit of him: but if ever Fate should bring together in the same Island, the remarker and the author, they may be better acquainted, for the latter will not wish to conceal himself from his angry friend the remarker. For the present, the Writer of the remarks; who is well known, and whose pen, driven on by his cacoethes scribendi, like a barber's scissars, is always snipping whether it cuts or not; will be permitted to ride his hobby-horse, in

full

full speed, uninterrupted; and to indulge, unmolested, his talent for controversy, which he takes naturally to, like fishes in India, that are said to have worms in their heads, and swim always against the stream.

A SHORT

History of Barbados.

Of its Situation, Settlement, and Government.

Barbados, the most considerable, and most windward of the Caribbee islands, extends from latitude 13 to 13. 20 N. and from longitude 58. 50 to 59. 3 W. from London, and is about thirty miles long, and twenty broad. Its situation gives it many advantages over the other Caribbees; particularly that of its being the first port where provision ships and others usually stop. It is strange that the English in general are

are so much in the dark as they are, with regard to their original possession of that valuable island: nor can it be otherwise accounted for, than by the first colonists being so much immersed in commercial pursuits, that they gave very little attention to matters of mere curiosity. Even the origin of its name is doubtful; some attributing it to a tree, whose distant appearance resembles a human beard. Others, perhaps with more probability, think, that it was first called Los Barbados by the Portuguese, from the barbarous uncultivated prospect it afforded.

The author of the Natural History of Barbados has laboured to prove, that this island was once inhabited by Indians; but his arguments are all conjectural; he tells us, that many Indian instruments and Indian huts, were found here by the first settlers; but we have not any certain

tain account of Indians having ever been difcovered in this ifland: nor any remains feen of the antient Caribbeans. It is not improbable, however, but thefe inftruments might have been brought hither, and thefe huts built, by the Portuguefe, who might have ftopt here in their voyages to and from Brazil.

When the Englifh firft difcovered Barbados, is not with certainty afcertained; but from the moft probable accounts we are led to conclude, it muft have been between the years 1615 and 1624. When the great fire happened in Bridge-Town in 1668, when many records were deftroyed, fome papers were preferved, which were afterwards printed; by thefe it appeared, that an Englifh fhip called the Olive, homeward bound from Guiney, touched there, and landed fome men, who fet up a crofs in or near St. James's

James's Town, and marked on a tree, "James king of England, and this island." Afterwards, about the year 1624, it is clear, from many authentic accounts, that a ship belonging to Sir William Courteen (one of the most considerable merchants in London) stopt at this island. About thirty of the crew landed, and made a settlement on the westward part of the island; although they found the country entirely uninhabited, and overgrown with thick woods.

They chose William Deane their leader, and erected the British colours upon the infant fortifications. At the return of this ship to England, the favourable report made of the island, induced Sir William Courteen and his friends to fit out two ships, with all kinds of necessaries for planting and fortifying this new acquired island; but his design

was

was no sooner known, than Hay Earl of Carlisle applied for and obtained a gift from the crown of all the Caribbee islands. This, however, did not prevent Courteen's ships from sailing; for the Earl of Carlisle happened at that time to be abroad upon an embassy; and Courteen availing himself of the earl's absence, prevailed on his friend and patron, the earl of Pembroke, to obtain from Charles I. a grant of this island, in trust for Courteen; in consequence of which, several adventurers went out in Courteen's ships.

When the earl of Carlisle returned from his embassy, he was surprized to hear of the settlement that had been made upon an island that was within his prior grant, and resolved to defeat it: to this end, he made an agreement with five or six merchants of London for ten thousand

thousand acres in the nature of a lease, to be settled under the direction of a person of their own chusing: the choice fell upon Charles Woolferstone, who went to Barbados with sixty-four persons, to whom the ten thousand acres had been ginated. Woolferstone, soon after his arrival, emitted a proclamation, in which he treated the Pembroke settlement as an usurpation, and summoned those settlers to appear at the Bridge-Town: they obeyed; and being few in number, submitted to Carlisle's authority.—The earl of Carlisle now applied to the throne to redress his grievances; complaining of the wrongs done him by Sir William Courteen.—The king hereupon annulled the grant to the earl of Pembroke; and gave to the earl of Carlisle a second patent, dated in April 1629, confirming the former, and explaining all doubts that had arisen thereto.

In 1629 the earl of Carlisle sent out colonel Henry Hawley, governor of Barbados, and though there were then but few inhabitants in the country, yet from this period to the government of Mr. Bell in 1641 (when the civil war drove great numbers of people from England thither) we find the island to have been continually in a state of mutiny and internal dissentions: owing to the arbitrary and violent disposition of Mr. Hawley, who was, at last, sent a prisoner to England, and his possessions seized by Henry Hunkes for treasonable practices.

The earl of Carlisle confirmed and approved the conduct of Hunkes, who assumed the command of this little colony until the year 1641, when the earl appointed Philip Bell lieutenant-governor of Barbados.

During the government of Mr. Bell, Barbados was settled, and a constitutional system established. Laws were framed for the security of property, and punishment of vice. Then it was that the calamities of England served to people Barbados. Then it was that this infant colony afforded a safe retreat to the inhabitants of her mother-country, where many families, antient and opulent, having expended their patrimony in support of monarchy, or having been plundered of their wealth by usurpers, sought in this distant isle the re-establishment of that fortune they had been robbed of, and the enjoyment of that peace they had been denied in their native land.——Thus was Barbados peopled and settled. [d] An old author, treating of this island, tells us, that Barbados was soonest peopled of all

[d] See vol. II. of the British Empire in America.

our colonies, and was settled by gentlemen of good families, and moderate fortunes.

To prove this assertion, we could here mention many of the first settlers, who were tempted to migrate hither, and make this colony their asylum; whose ancestors were seated with a comfortable affluence in different parts of England, and particularly in the counties of Cornwall, Devonshire, Stafford, Surry, Middlesex, Essex, Suffolk, Kent: but mankind are all of a race equally antient; and the business of history is not to follow whimsical genealogists, but to present objects, and relate facts, worthy to employ the attention of reasonable beings.

During this period the inhabitants increased so fast, that it was computed that in 1650 there were twenty thousand white men; and that the island could then muster ten thousand foot, and one thousand horse, for its defence. Governor Bell now thought of making proper regulations for the government of an island become so populous and important. He, by the advice of a council of his own appointing consisting of ten gentlemen, formed an assembly to represent the people. The island was divided into four circuits and eleven parishes.——The great increase of white men upon the island, occasioned a proportionable increase of blacks to cultivate the land: this colony therefore was obliged, like the French and Spaniards, to import from Africa large numbers of negroes. This was at that time a dangerous, because a new expedient. These negroes in a short time

time beheld themselves more numerous, and therefore they thought themselves more powerful, than their masters. Not being, as they afterwards were, and now are, habituated to the intercourse of Europeans, they soon entered into conspiracies: and so far were they hurried by a general spirit of discontent, that they even fixed upon a day for an universal rising; but the day before the massacre was to have taken place, one of the party discovered the plot to his master Mr. Hotherfall, who, by sending immediate notice to the inhabitants, prevented the execution of the conspiracy, and brought the offenders to justice.

It is probable, that the multiplicity of business of the British government about this period prevented that attention to the affairs of Barbados, which ought

ought to have been given to an infant colony. Mr. Bell continued to act under the proprietary commiffion, until Francis lord Willloughby not only obtained from Charles II. during his exile, a commiffion to be governor of Barbados, but alfo covenanted with the earl of Carlifle for a term of years, upon a certain confideration in the nature of a fee-farm rent, to be the proprietary governor likewife. In 1650 Francis lord Willoughby arrived at Barbados. He found the country flourifhing and populous, and the generality of the inhabitants well affected to the royal caufe. One of the firft fteps of his adminiftration was to fummon an affembly, which paffed an act, intituled, " An Acknowledgment and declaration " of the inhabitants of Barbados of " his majefty's right to the dominion " of this ifland, and the right of the
" earl

"earl of Carlisle derived from his said
"majesty; and also for the unanimous
"profession of the true religion in this
"island, and imposing condign punish-
"ment on the opposers thereof." The
governor also, assisted by the island,
acted with great spirit and success in
fitting out ships, and raising men, to
reduce the neighbouring islands under
his government to acknowledge the
loyal authority.

In the mean time it was notified to
the governor, to encourage him in the
cause, and to gain his assistance on the
occasion, that prince Rupert, who com-
manded the Royal fleet, intended to
sail to Barbados, and to secure all the
English American possessions for the
king. But this scheme being discovered in England, a powerful squadron
was equipt under the command of Sir
George

George Afcue, whose intention was to intercept prince Rupert, and to reduce Barbados, and the other islands in the West-Indies, to the obedience of the Commonwealth. Sir George cruized some time off Spain and Portugal, where he missed prince Rupert, and from whence he bent his course towards Barbados, and on the 16th of October 1651, he appeared off Bridge-Town with his squadron, and seized a few ships that were in Carlisle-bay; but he found the service he was sent upon more difficult than he imagined. The sight of such an hostile fleet was far from being agreeable to the inhabitants of a young colony, yet Lord Willoughby and the natives appeared determined to defend the island to the last extremity; and indeed the defence made upon this occasion is not to be wondered at; for, exclusive of the principle

ciple upon which that particular set of men acted, we shall find in general, that the inhabitants of distant colonies will more readily submit to the government of one, than many. The forts in Carlisle-bay protected that harbour so effectually, and so formidable a body of men assembled on the shore, that although Sir George had on board two thousand land forces, he could not effect his landing; but his squadron was kept beating about the island till December, when he anchored in Speight's bay; where (perceiving that his force was actually too small to reduce the island) he waited till the arrival of the Virginia merchant fleet, on board of which was a regiment of seven hundred men, and about one hundred and fifty Scotch transports: resolving to avail himself of this reinforcement, he immediately

mediately made difpositions for landing all his men. The landing was effected, and Afcue's forces gained the fort at Speight's-bay with four pieces of cannon; but they fuftained great lofs in the attack. Lord Willoughby kept the field; and though there was not any great probability of his effectually ferving the caufe he efpoufed, yet Afcue could make no impreffion upon his troops. At length Sir George Afcue offered to the inhabitants terms of peace that were mild and moderate. The planters, wearied out by the fatigue of the war, diftreffed too by the ruin of their eftates, whofe cultivation they were not allowed to attend to, and allured by the profpect of peace, liftened to the terms that were offered. A negotiation enfued. Many of the moft confiderable men of the ifland immediately declared for a peace. Lord Willoughby, thus apprized of the fentiments

of

of his friends, was obliged to agree to a ceffation of arms. Each party appointed four commiffioners, who, upon the 17th of January, agreed on articles of peace, alike comprehenfive and honourable: both parties were fecured in their freedom and property; as was lord Willoughby alfo, though he was obnoxious in the laft degree to the governing party in England. This moderation was of infinite fervice to Barbados; nor was the pacification followed by any acrimonious meafures againft the loyalifts. Lord Willoughby immediately embarked for Europe; and we hear no more of him till after the Reftoration.

Mr. Searl was now appointed governor of Barbados, and continued fo until the death of Cromwell; when the Committee of Safety (as it was called) affumed the direction of national affairs, and

and gave the government of that island to colonel Modiford; in whose time the assembly's continuance, was limited to one year.

About this time the act of navigation took place in England; this, with the duties soon afterwards laid upon the manufactures of this country, reduced much its wealth. At this period too the population of Barbados began in some measure to decrease, by the conquest of Jamaica, and the cultivation of other islands in America. Just before this, Barbados was so well inhabited, that in the expedition under Penn and Venables against Hispaniola, the Barbadians alone furnished three thousand five hundred soldiers; little fore-seeing, that the casual conquest of Jamaica would prove so prejudicial to them, as it afterwards did.

Charles II. being restored, and Hay Earl of Kinnnoul becoming heir to the Carlisle estate, the king proposed to give him one thousand pounds *per annum* for the surrender to the crown of the late earl of Carlisle's patent for the Carribbee islands. Kinnoul accepted the offer; and thus the proprietary government was dissolved, and Barbados reverted to the crown.

The king, willing to reward lord Willoughby for his former conduct, confirmed to him the government of Barbados, by a new commission, appointing him captain-general and governor in chief of this and the rest of the Caribbee islands for seven years, with a salary of twelve hundred pounds *per annum*. In this commission was inserted a new clause, giving to the king a power to approve

prove or disallow of all laws that should pass in that island. But the advantages Barbados was to reap from the dissolution of the proprietary government she was like to pay dear for. The planters were now told, that his majesty expected the legislature would grant him a proper consideration for the benefits they were to enjoy under a royal government. It was urged too, that the earl of Carlisle had died much in debt; and that his debts, together with the thousand pounds annuity granted to his heir, must be satisfied out of his patent. The demand was accordingly made. The Barbadians, not unmindful of their interest, appointed agents in England to remonstrate against this demand: but, alas! the agents were informed, that it was expected that Barbados would grant to the crown four and an half *per cent.* on the dead commodities of the produce of the island. The agents

agents replied, that this would amount to a tax of ten *per cent.* of the clear profits of the planters estates, and that it was a burden the country could not bear. The measure, however, had been resolved upon; and the king, as well as the dependents of his court, was so greatly interested in its success, that lord Willoughby agreed to carry it into execution, by going over himself to Barbados. But his lordship not going immediately, this affair slept for a short time; and the administration of affairs was left with Humphrey Walrond esq.—This gentleman discharged his duty with great integrity and prudence: many useful and beneficial acts were passed by the legislature during his administration; the good effects of which are yet felt and acknowledged.

In 1663 Francis lord Willoughby arrived again at Barbados. He found the

inhabitants of all degrees extremely out of humour with the tax that had been propoſed. The royaliſts thought it an ungrateful return for their ſufferings, and the others oppoſed it of courſe. This oppoſition gave the governor great diſquiet. He called an aſſembly four months after his arrival; and though the ſpirit of the people ran high againſt the propoſed tax, yet the aſſembly were prevailed with to comply; confirming to themſelves, by this purchaſe, the great charter of Britiſh ſubjects; and eſtabliſhing a permanent right to their poſſeſſions, which is expreſsly provided for by this law. However, they hoped, and intended, that ſeveral public charges of the country ſhould likewiſe be defrayed by this tax: induced chiefly by this conſideration, they paſſed an act with the following preamble: " As nothing conduceth
" more to the peace and proſperity of
" any

" any place, and the protection of every
" single person therein, than that the
" public revenue thereof may be in some
" measure proportioned to the public
" charges and expences; and also well
" weighing the great charges that there
" must be, of necessity, in maintaining
" the honour and dignity of his majesty's
" authority here, the public meeting of
" the sessions, the often attendance of
" the council, the reparation of the forts,
" the building a sessions-house and a pri-
" son, and all other charges incumbent
" on the government; we do, in conside-
" ration thereof, give and grant unto his
" majesty, his heirs and successors for
" ever, that is to say, upon all dead com-
" modities of the growth of this island,
" that shall be shipped off the same,"
&c. &c. From hence it appears, that
this tax (of the annual value of more than

twenty

twenty thoufand pounds to the crown) was granted and intended to be applied to the payment of all public charges for the fupport of the government of this ifland. If then the public charges and expences, fet forth in the above preamble, have been anfwered by this impoft, then the Barbadians have no reafon to complain: but if, on the contrary, thefe articles have not been complied with, furely the intent of this act hath not been anfwered, and the inhabitants have reafon to be difpleafed with it; and it may be obferved too, that this ifland was not originally acquired either by conqueft or purchafe; it is not therefore to be wondered at, that the inhabitants fhould think it in their power to apply the ufes of any money to be raifed, in fuch manner as they fhould judge proper. So ardent an oppofition was made to the paffing of this act, that lord Willoughby was apprehenfive of a general

general revolt. He ordered Mr. Farmer, a man of consequence in the opposition, to be arrested, and sent over prisoner to England, with a charge against him of mutiny, sedition, and treason: when Farmer arrived in England, he was brought before the king and council, where he pleaded with a freedom which the temper of that court could not bear, and which lord Clarendon called insolent, and deserving imprisonment. Farmer urged the rights of an Englishman; and that he had done nothing, but in a loyal, constitutional manner. His plea became his demerit, and he was sent to prison chiefly through the influence of Clarendon: nor did he recover his liberty till after a long tedious confinement. The frailties of mankind are visible in the wisest men: able as lord Clarendon was, his conduct towards Farmer must be acknowledged very severe. Thus was Mr, Farmer rewarded for his patriotism. From whence we may inforce this observation, that men are to take their lots in governments as in climates, to fence against the inconveniencies of both, and to bear what they cannot alter: for vain indeed will it be, to look for perfect governments in a world governed by such imperfect creatures as men.

The attention of the Barbadians was now called to the defence of their island. De Ruyter, the Dutch admiral, appeared off Barbados in 1664, with a design to make a descent upon that island, and did actually attack some of the forts in Carlisle bay; but he was so warmly received, and the Barbadians having drawn out their militia, made so good an appearance on the beach, that the Dutch squadron soon retired.

Two

Two years afterwards lord Willoughby undertook an expedition against the Dutch settlements to the southward: he appointed Henry Willoughby and Henry Hawley, esqrs. to be deputy-governors in his absence.—His lordship during this expedition perished by shipwreck. The new governors during their administration executed a very useful design. Their intentions were to reduce and ascertain the laws of the island, which stood much in need of a proper arrangement [e]. An act accordingly passed, which appointed commissioners to collect and amend what laws were in force, and these having received the royal assent, continue among the standing laws of the island to this day.

[e] The laws of Barbados are now become so voluminous, that a proper reduction and arrangement of them would be very useful to that island.

The

The death of Francis lord Willoughby being known in England, the king appointed his brother William lord Willoughby to succeed him in the government of Barbados. This governor brought with him from England a regiment of soldiers under the command of Sir Tobias Bridge; but we do not find how they were destined, or what use they were of to the country. In this administration many regulations were made in regard to the law courts of the island, and its internal police; an useful act passed also, declaring negro slaves to be real estate.

William lord Willoughby died in 1674, and his place as governor was the same year supplied from England by Sir Jonathan Atkins. Thus ended the government of these two lords.

Notwithstanding the just complaint against the duty of four and an half *per cent*. and the harsh proceedings against Farmer, it must be confessed, that the administrations of those two lords were prudent, and well calculated for the prosperity of a young colony. After the Restoration, the humour of preferring Jamaica to our other islands, which had been adopted during the Usurpation, subsided: and Barbados, latterly, recovered its strength so greatly under its last governor, that when Sir Jonathan Atkins arrived, the inhabitants were reckoned to be fifty thousand white men, and seventy thousand blacks or slaves; a number scarcely credible to be supported in so small an island. But a dreadful hurricane in August 1675 changed much the face of the country: to heighten this calamity

calamity too, New England was not in a condition at this time to send hither the usual supplies of provisions and timber; thus the crop of sugar being destroyed, added to the rapaciousness of creditors, many families were obliged to retire to other countries. The legislature, among many useful plans for the relief of their island, agreed to present an address to the government of Great Britain, praying that they may be relieved from the duty of four and an half *per cent.* as the only means of preserving their country from ruin: but this indulgence was denied them, and their petition failed of success. It was in vain for the Barbadians to remonstrate upon their hardships, and to complain that none of the public-spirited purposes, for which that great tax had been granted, had ever been answered. Thus Barbados shared not the

fate

fate of an elder child, the first offspring of her mother country, but was left to recover her losses as she could.

We find by the statutes of this island, that about this time some Quakers were very busy in their endeavours to convert the negro slaves: their principles of non-resistance were far from being agreeable to a colony, which, like that of Barbados, was every hour exposed to invasion; and therefore an act passed to prohibit negroes from frequenting meeting-houses: and the same act contained a clause against Dissenters, to prevent their teaching pupils, and keeping schools upon the island. This was a precaution perhaps not impolitic in a colony, where labour was of more utility than learning.

Sir Jonathan Atkins being recalled was succeeded in April 1680 by Richard Dutton,

Dutton, esq. in whose commission the members [f] of his majesty's council were

[f] The members of council were:

Henry Walrond,
John Reide,
Timothy Thornhill,
John Gibbes,
Francis Bond,
John Farmer,
George Lillington, } Esqrs.

George Andrews,
William Sharpe,
Tobias Frere,
Michael Terril,
The Reverend Mr. William Walker. } Esqrs.

The members of the assembly about this period were:

Parish	Members	
S. Mich. Parish	George Peers, William Wheeler,	Esqrs.
Christ Church	Thomas Maxwell, Daniel Hooper,	Esqrs.
S. Philip's	William Fortescue, Henry Markland,	Esqrs.
S. John's	John Leslie, James Colleton,	Esqrs.
S. George's	Richard Salter, Miles Toppin,	Esqrs.
S. Joseph's	John Holder, Henry Gollop,	Esqrs.
S. Andrew's	William Dottin, Richard Walter,	Esqrs.
S. Thomas's	Jonathan Downes, Thomas Sadlier,	Esqrs.
S. James's	Abel Alleyne, William Holder,	Esqrs.
S. Peter's	Samuel Maynard, Robert Harrison,	Esqrs.
S. Lucy's	Thomas Merrick, John Gibbes,	Esqrs.

first

firſt inſerted: a practice, we apprehend, that hath been continued ſince. The governor immediately iſſued writs to elect an aſſembly. This gentleman was received with great kindneſs and reſpect by the inhabitants; for which he made a very ungenerous return. He was tyrannical and oppreſſive; and his deſpotiſm was ſo great, that many families, unable to endure his tyrannic ſway, quitted their country: this induced the legiſlature to paſs an act for regulating the manner of giving tickets out of the ſecretary's office. In 1684 an act paſſed to appoint a treaſurer of the iſland; and this office was conferred upon Mr. Salter. At this time too the militia was regulated and ſettled by the law. The rebellion in the weſt of England breaking out about this time, the legiſlature paſſed a ſevere act againſt thoſe rebels that were ſent to Barbados, whereby their condition was

ren-

rendered almoſt equal to a ſtate of ſlavery.

About this period a complaint was lodged in England againſt Henry Walrond, eſq. a member of council, for a petty charge againſt him, on account of a trial before a court of oyer and terminer, in which Walrond preſided as chief juſtice. After a full trial at an aſſize in England, he was only fined thirty pounds; but his detention there, and the expences of his ſuit (his adverſary being vigorouſly ſupported by the governor) hurt much his fortune. At his return to Barbados, the council and aſſembly preſented to him five hundred pounds, as an acknowledgement of his former ſervices to his country; and added a declaration of his juſt proceedings at the court of oyer.

In

In 1685 an additional duty was laid upon sugar; a burden upon the planters which confiderably reduced the value of their plantations. It could not fail to fill the world with aftonifhment, to obferve that the colonies, which brought fuch wealth to the mother country, nurfing her failors, and increafing her manufacturers, fhould be fingled out as the hunted ftag, and their inhabitants overloaded with taxes. The Barbadians reprefented their grievances to the government of Great Britain. They faid, that if a tax muft be laid upon trade, it might be laid upon all commodities alike; that a fmall advance upon all the cuftoms would ferve every purpofe, as well as a great one upon fome; and that this could be borne with more eafe, there being a larger number to partake of it. All their remonftrances availed them not any thing. Governor Dutton encouraged

couraged every motion to diftrefs the planters; and was fo zealous a friend to the Royal African Company (which had much hurt Barbados), that when he went to England he appointed Edwin Stede his deputy-governor, who was only an agent to the African Company, and fecretary to the governor. Stede had however the addrefs to eftablifh a precedent, which has ever fince been adopted: he prevailed with the legiflature to prefent him with one thoufand pounds; from whence it became cuftomary to make prefents to the governors, who before this had only their Englifh falary. About this time was a confpiracy of the negroes; which however was foon difcovered and ftopt: this occafioned many useful acts to be paffed for the government of negroes.

Soon

Soon after the Revolution, king William appointed James Kendal, esq. governor of Barbados; who, soon after his arrival there, transmitted to England very satisfactory accounts of the loyalty and good disposition of this colony: so that the Revolution was productive of no change in Barbados; but all its inhabitants chearfully and willingly acknowledged king William: they loved monarchy, conscious that it was an essential part of the excellent constitution of their mother country; but they knew too, that the preservation of that constitution, and the happiness of that country, required that a Protestant king should wear the crown.

During this administration the inhabitants of St. Christopher, and the other Leeward islands, being much distressed by the French, applied to Barbados for assistance: the Barbadians readily complied with their request; and Timothy Thornhill, esq. having offered his service, received a commission from the legislature to raise a regiment: this regiment amounted to seven hundred men, who were all cloathed, armed, and embarked in transport ships for St. Christophers at the expence of this colony: this expedition took place in August 1689: the Barbadians also raised two regiments more of five hundred men each to assist the expedition against Martinique, and which joined the troops from England under the command of Colonel Foulks [g]: according to the best accounts, this invasion was miserably mismanaged; what little effectual service was performed, the troops of Barbados and the Leeward islands

[g] For the particulars of these expeditions, see the British Empire in America, vol. ii.

claimed

claimed the merit of. The 24th of January 1693, governor Kendal received information that nine French ships of war were plying to the north east of the island: he immediately, with the advice of the council, ordered two merchant ships to be taken into their majesty's service, and fitted as men of war; these joined their majesty's ships the Norwich, the Mary, the Antelope, the Mordaunt, the Diamond, and two sloops, which were then in Carlisle-bay under the command of captain Wren: this fleet sailed the 30th of January, and returned the 5th of February, not having seen the enemy; however they sailed again in a few days, in search of the French squadron, with whom they engaged the 17th of February to leeward of Martinique. Both squadrons claimed the victory, and Captain Wren returned with all his ships to Carlisle-bay. At this time the

freight

freight of sugar ran so high, and masters of ships were so exorbitant in their demands, that the legislative power was obliged to interfere, and by an act of the island regulate the freight of its commodities. This act was afterwards repealed.

In 1694 Mr. Kendal was recalled, and the honourable Francis Russel was appointed governor of Barbados, where he arrived with his family the same year. The council and assembly presented their new governor with two thousand pounds, and the following year gave him two thousand more. These expences caused great murmurings among the people, who became alarmed at such mischievous precedents. In truth, the governors became now to be a sort of grievance by these exactions of money, which they appeared to look for as their right; forgetting that such gifts flow only from the benevolence of the inhabitants. The governor, council and assembly now transmitted a very loyal address of condolance to his majesty king William on the death of his royal consort queen Mary, which was presented by Willoughby Chamberlyne, esq. and graciously received.

In 1696 governor Russel died; and Francis Bond, esq. the senior member of the council, became president and commander in chief. This gentleman's administration was productive of many wise measures for the benefit of his country. Many useful laws were passed, which remain yet in force. The inhabitants were easy, and perfectly satisfied with their president: and, in truth, we shall always find, that a man who both has an interest in a country, and is a native thereof,

thereof, will be more concerned for the good government of it, and more attentive to its prosperity, than one who considers it as a temporary dwelling, whither he has procured himself to be sent to raise a fortune, or to patch up one going to decay.

In 1698 his majesty was pleased to appoint the honourable Ralph Grey (afterwards lord Grey) governor of Barbados, where he arrived the 26th of July. An act soon passed, presenting Mr. Grey with two thousand pounds, and five hundred pounds for the rent of an house; Fontabelle house (the governor's residence) being much out of repair. Governor Grey's administration was very popular. The Barbadians, naturally hospitable and generous, love a governor possessed of these qualities. Mr. Grey was generous and magnificent, which endeared him to Barbados;

Barbados; a disinterested disposition, and a particular attention to the welfare of that island, marked him a man of worth, who did not wish, through avaricious views, to distress the country he was sent to protect. His health declining, he was obliged to leave his government in 1701, when the command devolved upon [h] John Farmer, esq. the senior member of council; in whose time happened the death of king William, and the accession of queen Anne. Events which were notified in form.

In 1703 Sir Bevill Granville arrived at Barbados governor thereof: a new house was immediately built for Sir Bevill upon a spot called Pilgrim-hill, which continues to this day to be the governor's house: the assembly, soon after the

[h] Son of Mr. Farmer, who was sent to England by lord Willoughby.

governor's arrival, was so complaisant, as to appoint his brother one of their agents in England; a conduct courtly indeed, but not very politic; for the governor's brother was wholly unacquainted with that island, and its concerns: and an agent ought to be a man well versed in the constitution of the country he serves, and who perfectly understands her true interest: attentive only to his agency, he should watch for occasions to be beneficial to the country, with whose welfare he is entrusted: establishing an interest with the board of trade, he should never be ignorant of what is doing at that office: well acquainted with business, he should endeavour to connect himself with, and have a perfect knowledge of, the forms, rules, and methods of the different offices he must transact business with. It is much to be wished too, for the benefit of Barbados, that the agent could always

always be a member of the British parliament, as his consequence would then be much enlarged, and he would probably claim a more respectful attention from the ministry.

The frequent presents to governors having caused much uneasiness to the inhabitants, and having truly been found to be distressful to the island, her majesty was pleased to augment the governor's English salary from twelve hundred to two thousand pounds *per annum*. During Sir Bevill Granvill's administration Barbados was miserably distressed by factions. Party raged high. Complaints were sent to England against the governor by those in the opposition. Remonstrances followed from his friends; but we do not find, however, that any regard was paid to either. In the year 1705 the assembly, taking into consideration the
great

great want of cash in the island, passed an act to allow sixty-five thousand pounds paper credit; impowering Mr. Holder the treasurer (who was also speaker of the assembly) to give out bills for that sum. The men of greatest property in the island opposed this scheme with great violence, but with little effect. This act was severely censured in England, and repealed immediately. The governor, dissatisfied with his situation, obtained his recall, and died upon his voyage home. In Sir Bevill's administration St. Ann's Castle was built in honor of her majesty; which, from its situation, seems well calculated to annoy an enemy.

In 1707 Mitford Crow, esq. arrived at Barbados, governor of the island. He, in obedience to his instructions, removed all those gentlemen from the council, and from all other offices which they held

under

under the crown, who were concerned in promoting the paper credit act. This spread so much discontent in the country, and rendered Mr. Crow's situation so irksome, that it was soon thought proper to recall him also.

He was succeeded in 1711 by Robert Lowther, esq. who was twice governor of Barbados. His first administration lasted till 1714, when he was recalled, and Mr. Sharpe, the senior member of the council, became president. In 1713 the legislature passed a very judicious act, by which was settled, the proportion of water, to be used by each Proprietor of the lands, through which a spring, called Three-houses spring, ran; the head of this spring is deemed to arise in a public road in St. Philip's parish: thus was this bounty of Heaven impartially distributed, and not suffered to be monopolized by any particular

cular person. In 1715 his majesty was pleased to appoint Mr. Lowther again to this government. Both periods of his administration were very unpopular, displeasing to himself, and disagreeable to the inhabitants. Parties were early formed against him, which always galled him during his nine years residence upon the island; yet he both times gained a handsome settlement. During his first administration he suspended three members of council, Mr. Sharpe, Mr. Walker, and Mr. Berisford. The queen took off their suspension. They were nevertheless withheld for some short time from setting in council [1], which consequently stopt the course of business, and was thereby of the utmost prejudice to the country.

[1] In the Caribbeana, published in 1741, is a very sensible opinion of Mr. Codrington, relative to this suspension.

How-

However, the three members at length re-assumed their seats, and nothing more was heard of this matter. During his second admistration many complaints from time to time were exhibited against him; particularly for his persecution of the reverend Mr. Gordon, rector of St. Michael's parish, and the bishop's commissary; against whom some harsh proceedings having passed, Gordon appealed to the crown. He obtained from the lords justices (his majesty being then at Hanover) an order to take depositions at Barbados; and the governor (who was the accuser) had the same privilege. Gordon returned to Barbados, and served this order upon the governor, who paid so little regard to it, that he committed Gordon prisoner to the common gaol. At the court of oyer, where Gordon was tried, the governor presided. This step, though very unusual, is nevertheless agreeable to law. Such were the measures of this court, that the governor even prosecuted the council and attorney who appeared in behalf of Gordon: the former went to England, and presented these proceedings with proper complaints against the governor; which had so good an effect, that the lords justices (in the king's absence) sent to Barbados an order conceived in the strongest terms against the governor, ordering that the proceedings at that court in this affair, should all be vacated. In consequence of this and other complaints Mr. Lowther was recalled. He left the island in May 1720; but before his departure he suspended Samuel Cox, esq. the eldest member of the council; and John Frere, esq. the next member of council, became president. Soon after this, Sir Charles Cox petitioned the king

against

against governor Lowther, for having removed his brother from the council in an illegal and arbitrary manner; and his majesty was pleased to send an order to Mr. Frere to resign the command to Mr. Cox: but by some means or other this order was not complied with; and Sir Charles Cox enforcing his complaints, Mr. Frere was summoned to appear before the king and council of Great Britain: he accordingly in 1721 resigned the government to Mr. Cox, much against the inclinations of the inhabitants of Barbados. He immediately went to England, where he was given to understand, that his being sent for was to place him out of Cox's way, and to break the violence of party.

Mr. Cox acceded to the government of Barbados at a time when party raged high against him. The tranquillity act had

had passed; the design of which was to keep all officers, &c, in their places in spite of the president's power [k]: and all the chief offices of the island were filled with Cox's enemies; so that, when he took possession of the command, he was so hampered by the opposition, that he thought himself obliged to have recourse to a very extraordinary step: he suspended five members of council at one time, and swore in five others in their places. The suspended members were immediately restored by the crown: a circumstance of such triumph to that party, that they exulted more than ever, and perplexed the affairs of government so much, that even the excise bill, which was absolutely necessary for the support of the public, was in danger of being lost. It must be owned too, that Mr. Cox did not be-

[k] This act was repealed.

have with requisite moderation: he removed from the bench of justices several gentlemen of fortune, particularly Guy Ball, esq. a member of the council, and had endeavoured to commence vexatious prosecutions against them: he attempted to prosecute Judge Sutton, who he charged with having written to him, with ill manners, and disrespect; but the king's Attorney General Richard Carter esq. refused to enter a prosecution, declaring the charge was not sufficient to ground an indictment, or information upon; and adding, that, by the law of all civilized nations, if even a Prince does require something to be done, which the person who is to do it takes to be unlawful, it is not only lawful, but his duty, *rescribere principi*; and should he carry on a prosecution by indictment or information, against the king's subjects, which may hereafter come to be adjudged unlawful in a proper place, and for which he may be put to anſwer, it would not be ſufficient juſtification for him to ſay, he had the Preſident's order grounded upon the opinions of five members of the council [1]. In conſequence of the abuſe Mr. Cox made of his power, in all ſubſequent inſtructions from the crown the authority of preſidents was much limited, and their power reduced to what it is at preſent. It is aſtoniſhing, that in ſo ſmall a ſpot, party-rage ſhould grow to ſuch an exceſs: never was any country more torn to pieces by parties, than Barbados was about this period: but, alas! we find faction and its ill conſequences prevailing in almoſt all countries; and in theſe little communities, where not any gain is acquired, vanity operates, as venality does in great ſtates.

[1] See Mr. Carter's Memorial in Vol. I. of the Caribbeana.

His majesty, willing to relieve the distresses of Barbados, in 1722 appointed Henry Worsley, esq. governor of that island, and gave him instructions and power to enquire into the conduct of president Cox, and to decide thereon as he should judge most proper. Governor Worsley, when he arrived at Barbados, conducted himself with so much policy, that neither party thought him their enemy; and therefore both parties courted him for their friend, and both were equally flattered by the governor. Each side made him large offers; and thus was the assembly brought to give him the enormous revenue of six thousand pounds *per annum*. The governor, having gained this great point, and the heavy tax of two shillings and six-pence being laid upon each negro for defraying this salary, he proceeded to enquire into the ſtate of the iſland before his acceſſion. He ſummoned Mr. Cox to a formal trial; and he determined, that Mr. Cox had acted, during his preſidentſhip, corruptly, arbitrarily, and illegally; and therefore he not only removed him from being of his majeſty's council, but alſo declared him incapable of ever being a member of that board [m].

This adminiſtration was marked by the death of his majeſty king George I. The Barbadians had very ſeverely felt their diſtreſs, occaſioned by the burdenſome ſalary given to the governor, which, in truth, had much oppreſſed that whole iſland: they therefore ſeized the opportunity of the king's death, as a plea to ſave their money, by refuſing to pay the tax of two ſhillings and ſix-pence laid

[m] Mr. Cox paſſed the remainder of his life upon the continent of N. America.

upon negroes; afferting, that by the king's death the governor's commiffion ceafed, and confequently the law which provided for the maintenance of the governor became void. But this fallacy did not fucceed, though it caufed much diforder in the country. Mr. Worfley prefented a memorial to the throne, in confequence of which his majefty was pleafed to direct (agreeable to the opinion of his attorney and folicitor general) "that in "cafe the arrears of the faid tax was "not paid on or before the 1ft day of "July next, that his majefty's attorney "general of Barbados do caufe proper "law-fuits to be commenced againft all "perfons liable to pay fuch arrears, &c." and thefe arrears were accordingly recovered. About this period, the duke of Portland, who had been appointed governor of Jamaica, landed at Barbados with his dutchefs and a fplendid retinue;

and these noble visitants departed from thence, highly pleased with the elegance, politeness, and hospitality of the Barbadians.

Mr. Worsley left the government of Barbados in 1731, and Samuel Berwick, esq. president of the council, succeeded him. Mr. Berwick (as several of his predecessors had done) executed his commission without any salary or present from the assembly, during the short time he presided.

He died the year following, and James Dottin esq. the next member of council, became commander in chief. The legislature, by an act of the island, settled four hundred pounds *per annum* upon Mr. Dottin; a proof at what an easy expence the business of this government was then carried on.

In

In 1733 lord viscount Howe was appointed governor of Barbados: he arrived in that island the same year. The legislature settled four thousand pounds upon his lordship: a large sum indeed for the circumstances of the island at that time! but which, however, the governor generously expended in the island. The universal good character of this nobleman filled every heart with joy upon his arrival: his lordship did not disappoint the hopes and expectations of Barbados. By a generosity of temper, and a complacency of deportment; by an equitable distribution of justice, and a steady adherence to the constitution and true interest of the country he presided over, he preserved the island free from faction, and gained the affection and esteem of all the inhabitants. So pacific a period affords little matter for history to transmit. The good agreement between the governor, council, and assembly, produced the best effects for the mother country, as well as for the colony; and surely never was there an experiment made with so much success, of what importance the right choice of a governor is to the prosperity of this, or any other of our sugar islands; yet it has been said, that, if this nobleman had lived a few years longer, he would have ruined Barbados by the introduction of luxury: but alas! experience hath fully taught us, that if the inhabitants of that country possess the means of indulging luxurious dissipation, the practice will be obtained in the mother country, if the times forbid the enjoyment of it in their native isle: but (for a moment) suppose the charge to be, in some degree, true; was it not an honest policy in the governor, to divert in

pleasures

pleasures and amusements that wealth which had formerly so often kindled the flames of party? Lord Howe died in March 1735; the council and assembly (applauded by all their countrymen) to testify their grateful remembrance of his lordship, as well as to distinguish merit, presented two thousand five hundred pounds to lady Howe.

Mr. Dottin succeeded again to the command, and received a settlement of six hundred pounds *per annum:* his administration was gentle and inoffensive.

In 1739 the honourable Robert Byng was appointed governor of Barbados, where he arrived soon after his appointment. The times were unfavourable to Mr. Byng. He came to the government at a time when the house of representatives seemed pertinaciously devoted, to the will of their speaker Henry Peers, esq. a gentleman a gentleman who had been difappointed in his hope of procuring the government of Barbados for himfelf, and whofe imaginary intereft and real intention it was, to diftrefs the new governor. " From men" (fays the great Sully) " all " things may be expected: they are not " to be kept firm to their duty, inte- " grity, and the laws of fociety, by fi- " delity and virtue, but by their hopes " and wifhes." Mr. Byng was by the firft addrefs of the affembly, as well as by private conferences, entertained with declamations of the poverty of Barbados, and the ftedfaft refolutions of its reprefentatives concerning his appointment, " which, they faid, could not be equal to " his predeceffors. The governor obferved, " that the country was now in a more " flourifhing condition than his prede- " ceffor found it in; he was confcious of " having brought with him as good in- " tentions

"tentions as the best of his predecessors;
"but that if he was less considered than
"his immediate predecessor, he could
"not avoid thinking it was setting an
"ignominious mark upon him; an in-
"dignity under which he could not sit
"easy." But he could not obtain more
than two thousand pounds *per annum*;
yet, to render this more palatable, an
additional present was added of two
thousand five hundred pounds to repair
the governor's losses at sea, the ship in
which his baggage was, having been
taken by the Spaniards. This was certainly an act of generosity in the assembly; but it did not heal the breach between the governor and speaker, which was now notorious, and faction again reared its hydra-head with its usual violence. [n] At length the speaker was

[n] Henry Peers, esq. speaker of the assembly, was lieutenant general, master general of the ordnance,

stript

stript of all the posts which he held under the crown. A circumstance that

president of the council of war, colonel of a regiment of militia, and a justice of peace. He was succeeded as lieutenant general, master general of the ordnance, and president of the council of war, by Thomas Applewhaite, esq. one of the members of his majesty's council, and who had been major general and colonel of the Windward regiment: these two gentlemen were many years contemporaries. They both gained honour and reputation in their country, but with very different tempers, they attached themselves early to opposite parties, and frequently espoused contending interests: yet, strange to say! they lived together in a close intimacy. Mr. Peers had good sense, and strong natural abilities, and acquired a peculiar dexterity in the management of a party. His fondness of power plunged him deep in faction. He was every man's enemy that opposed his party, and was often served through fear. His passions were impetuous and unmanageable. He was generous, lively, sanguine, intrepid, ambitious. In friendship warm. in resentment implacable. He claimed the title of a great man. By his death a powerful party lost their friend

affords

affords a remarkable æra in this administration. Mr. Peers died soon after, and tranquillity was re-assuming its empire throughout the island, when death snatched from the world the governor himself. Mr. Byng's administration was short and active. He lived only ten months in Barbados. His resolution and activity; his laborious turn for business, and an indefatigable application which nothing could divert; his attention to the defence of the island he command-

and patron. Mr. Applewhite possessed a sound judgment, and an amiable disposition, and was too candid and disinterested for the intrigues of faction. His moderation disengaged him from the inconveniencies of party-zeal. He was every man's friend that needed his friendship, and men were attached to him by affection. His passions were under the command of his reason. He was compassionate, affable, sincere, calm, resolute. In friendship steady: in resentment placable All men, with an united voice, called him a good man. By his death the poor lost their father and support.

ed, by forming its militia, and repairing its fortifications; and his schemes for the extention of trade; joined to his prudent discernment, which produced the best commission of the peace ever issued in that island, led many to regret the death of a governor, of whom they had entertained great expectations, notwithstanding the early opposition he encountered º.

Soon after Mr. Byng's death, the assembly unanimously agreed to the follow-

---

º Mr. Byng's good sense shewed itself very strong in this remarkable instance. The assembly presented an address to him of the 8th of July 1740, which, from a previous knowledge, he thought was extremely severe and unkind towards him: he, nevertheless, with a gracious smile, received it, made no reply to it, but with great cordiality and apparent friendship, caressed the assembly-men who presented it, and all others that fell in his way; and actually did give a lucrative employment to one of them the next day.

ing resolves: 1. That as many disadvantages and mischiefs have been found to arise, by means of the settlements made by the general assembly on governors, this house is now absolutely determined not to make any settlement whatever on any future governor: and that every member of this present assembly, while he continues in that trust, will steadily and unalterably abide by this resolution, notwithstanding any plausible reasons, or pretences, that may be urged to induce him to alter the same. And this house eanestly recommends, and hopes all future assemblies will comply therewith. 2. That an humble address be made to his most excellent majesty, humbly beseeching him to give directions, that such a salary for the future governors may be assigned, and paid out of the duty of four and half *per cent.* arising on the produce of this island, as may be sufficient for

their

their support, and the dignity of this government; and most humbly to entreat his majesty to discontinue the instruction permitting and allowing the assembly to make an additional settlement on any governor. And that an humble representation be also made to the lords commissioners for trade and plantations, praying their lordships endeavours to promote, and get established, what is implored of his majesty.

In 1740 Mr. Dottin again became president, and continued so until the arrival of Sir Thomas Robinson in 1742.

When Sir Thomas Robinson arrived at Barbados, an unusual shyness prevailed in the assembly towards their new governor. Though the preceding assembly had resolved not to make any settlement whatever upon a future governor: nevertheless,

less, the then assembly granted to Sir Thomas three thousand pounds *per annum*. The inimitable Sully, the ablest politician, and (what is more to his honour) the most unprejudiced man that history furnishes us with an account of, remarks, " that the " word Parliament carries with it an idea of " equity, and even wisdom; yet in these " bodies we meet with such instances of " irregularity, that one cannot help con- " cluding, that, if infallibility may be " hoped for among men, it will be found " rather in one than a multitude." To Sir Thomas Robinson, Barbados is indebted for an excellent armoury, the best in the West Indies, which he built at his own expence, and the utility of which that island hath experienced ever since; yet this armoury, and some alterations of Pilgrim-house, which were undertaken without the knowledge, and executed without the concurrence of the assembly, raised many contentions and disputes, between the governor and that body, which never subsided: and the assembly refused to pay for what they had not directed: the Governor was at length recalled.

Sir Thomas remained at Barbados until the arrival of his successor the honourable Henry Grenville in 1747. The council and assembly settled three thousand pounds *per annum* upon Mr. Grenville, whose administration was during the calm of peace, consequently not very interesting. In this administration the legal interest of money was reduced by law from eight to six *per cent.* a very useful measure for the country, because, the annual produce of plantations having decreased, the people were less able to pay a large interest; and experience proved, that their estates were unequal to an eight *per cent.* interest: a circumstance alone that

that must always overbalance the advantages of credit, which high interest affords a country; for what advantage could a planter derive from a loan, if he had not a prospect of repaying it? The Barbadians, taught by experience the mischievous effects of party, united to render Mr. Grenville's situation agreeable to himself, which his address rendered not displeasing to them. Abroad, he maintained the honour of his royal master, particularly by the successful effort he made to prevent the French from settling Tobago, then a neutral island. At home, unattached to any faction, he supported his commission with a pompous state; and though all confessed the haughtiness of the man, they could not but admire the dignity of the governor. In governments, as well as in courts, all things are brought about by artifice. The governor had the success, at the close of his administration,

tion, to obtain those public marks of approbation, which were never before lavished upon any governor; for so far did the then assembly proceed in their professions of esteem to this gentleman, that they voted a statue of him (one member only dissenting) to be erected in the town-hall, where the courts of justice are held, in honour to his memory, and to exemplify to posterity a pattern of justice and integrity [p]. Mr. Grenville

[p] The only persons intrusted by the governor with his secret wishes for a statue were John Fairchild esq. representative for St. Michael's parish, and William Duke esq. clerk of the assembly, these influenced the then assembly. John Lyte esq. representative for St. George's parish, and his friends, were thought to be not well affected to the governor: Ralph Weekes esq. (who was to succeed to the command of the island) was therefore prevailed upon to resign the judgeship of Ostin's court, which was given to Lyte; thus was he and his party appeased: the compliment intended the governor was a picture; when this was mentioned in the house, a member moved for a statue: the house consented.

continued

continued governor of Barbados till May 1753, when he applied for, and obtained, leave to return to England.

Ralph Weekes, esq. the senior member of the council, was then invested with the command. The assembly gave him twelve hundred pounds *per annum*, to support the honour and dignity of the king's commission: He was a good president, and preserved the affairs of government in their usual channel.

In August 1756 Charles Pinfold, esq; governor of Barbados, arrived in that island. He obtained a settlement of three thousand pounds *per annum*. A quiet, easy governor suits best a colony; such was Mr. Pinfold, whose qualities, however, were of the negative kind. His administration was long and interesting. His constant attention to the business of the court of chancery was truly meritorious; so regular was his attendance, and so assiduous was he to expedite the business of that court, that when he left the island, there was not one cause upon the chancery list ripe for hearing. During this period the Barbadians bore no inconsiderable share in the glorious events which distinguished the British arms during the last war. A resolution having been formed in England to reduce the island of Martinique (the key of the Caribbees), the same was communicated to the governor of Barbados. The governor immediately called together the council and assembly, and having communicated this intelligence, a law passed for assisting his majesty's forces; when the inhabitants, regardless of the injury their trade must receive, and which it afterwards did receive, by the acquisition of the large and valuable

island

island of Martinique, gave their assistance with a zeal, unanimity, and spirit, scarcely to be paralleled. Five hundred and eighty-eight white men (volunteers) were expeditiously raised, cloathed, and paid by the country; to these were added five hundred and eighty-three negroes. They joined his majesty's forces, and assisted at the reduction of Martinique. This expedition cost Barbados [q] twenty four thousand pounds currency, besides a large supply of provisions, which the Barbadians sent to the forces while they were besieging the enemy. During this administration the stamp act passed the parliament of Great Britain. This act threatened a precedent big with fatal

[q] Ten thousand pounds (sterling) were repaid by the government. The difference of exchange between Great Britain and Barbados is thirty-five *per cent.*

mischief;

mischief; yet this colony submitted to its validity, and trusting to the equity of the British legislature for its repeal, when its pernicious tendency should be perceived, was content with remonstrating against its oppression. This act was soon repealed; but during the few months it was in force, the sum of two thousand five hundred pounds was collected at Barbados, and remitted to England. Governor Pinfold, having obtained leave to return to England, embarked on board the Britannia, capt. Davis, the 27th of May 1766.

Samuel Rous esq. the senior member of council, then resident upon the island, acceded to the command, and took the oaths of office immediately after the departure of the governor. The council and assembly settled fifteen hundred pounds *per annum* upon the president during

during his residence at Pilgrim-house; nor do we find that this gentleman hath proved himself unworthy of the generosity of his countrymen. He hath supported his station, with a splendor and magnificence, equal to the unusual largeness of his salary, and hath acquitted himself in other respects to the satisfaction of his country, notwithstanding he has been engaged in a point of some delicacy, with the present speaker of the assembly. John Gay Alleyne, esq. having been chosen speaker of the house of representatives, and approved of by the commander in chief, immediately claimed from the king's representative the allowance of certain privileges, which he alledged the representatives of the people were intitled to. These privileges are:

First, Exemption from arrests to themselves and servants.

Secondly,

Secondly, Liberty of speech.

Thirdly, Access at all times to the king's representative.

To this demand the president said, "He would give his answer at the next "sitting of the assembly," cautiously taking time for consideration and advice: and his answer being at length given, was [r], "I give and grant, as far as is con-
"sistent with the royal prerogative,
"and the laws and constitution of this
"island, every privilege and liberty
"which hath been enjoyed by any for-

---

[r] In the first edition this answer was represented in other terms (though the meaning was not very different): this was owing to misinformation; which, the distance of place, and the difficulty of gathering materials, will, it is hoped, excuse.

"mer

" mer affembly, to be enjoyed by you,
" as fully and freely as ever." The obfervations that arife from this anfwer are too obvious to be illuftrated here: however, it is but juftice to acknowledge, that it was the moft fenfible and judicious the prefident could have given: for if he had abfolutely and unrefervedly granted the demand, he might (and perhaps with juftice too) have been cenfured by the government in England; and indeed fuch grant muft have been confirmed by a higher power than the prefident's, before it could have had effect: on the other hand, had he rejected the demand entirely, the remaining fhort period of his adminiftration might have been imbittered by diffentions and difputes: but his referve was prudent; he granted every privilege that had been enjoyed by any former affembly. What privilege or liberty had ever been granted or enjoyed by

by a former affembly? None. What then was granted to the prefent? Surely none. But with this anfwer the fpeaker retired feemingly well content; and moft likely he was really fo; he had gained the much-wifhed-for opportunity of haranguing, and of dazzling the eyes of the world, with a glare of patriotifm [f].

[f] Here it may be neceffary to obferve, that the cuftom of the fpeaker's afking for privileges is an act of his own, upon which he cannot be fuppofed to take any inftructions from the houfe, for after the choice of a fpeaker, the houfe by the rules of parliament can do no bufinefs until he has been approved, at other times indeed he delivers himfelf by command of the houfe. from hence the reafon will appear, why, in treating of thefe privileges, the fpeaker is confidered as diftinct from the houfe, and what is faid of him made applicable only to himfelf. See farther, Preface to Privileges of Jamaica, page 19.

In regard to the privileges thus demanded, it may be observed, that the exemption from arrests was never claimed, confequently never poffeffed, by any preceding affembly. If is meant an exemption from arrefts at all times, the precedent muft have a fatal tendency to affect the credit of Barbados, nor would the injury be much lefs prejudicial, if confined to the day of the affembly's fitting; for, under the protection of fervants, may not the power be given to fcreen from debt, and to find an opportunity to convey from off the ifland, a number of flaves? The police of Barbados is not altogether fimilar to that of Great-Britain: but even if it was, how could the community in general, by any means, be benefited by their reprefentatives being exempt from arrefts?

In a sister-colony, the council and assembly claim this privilege of exemption from arrests to their persons, servants, and equipages [t]: A representative's coach-horses were seized; the officers, who levied upon the horses, were committed by the speaker of the house. The prisoners applied to the governor (as chancellor) for an habeas corpus; the governor granted it, and they were released; the assembly was soon after dissolved. The new assembly re-committed the officers, as they conceived the court of chancery had no right to interfere; but the officers were again released as before; and thus this matter continued unsettled, until a new assembly was chosen in the year 1765, which remained silent as to the officers, and made no attempt to

[t] Privileges of Jamaica, Preface, page 5 [a], page 8 [b], page 15.

commit

commit them a third time; but they addressed the governor to expunge the record of his determination: this was refused, and their disputes were revived. Whether this governor did well or ill in the part he acted, is not for us to determine; possibly the most unexceptionable method of releasing the prisoners would have been by a prorogation, or dissolution of the assembly; but be this as it may, this circumstance is mentioned to shew, how the creditor must have suffered in acquiring his legal demand, and how the officers must have suffered in executing the duties of their office, if some power had not interfered; a power which ought surely to be lodged somewhere, as a check upon the exorbitant use of this privilege, a use ('tis too true) that might always be made of it, in any country whatever. Now, if a creditor hath no other method of coming

at his legal debt, and the seizure of servants or equipage should be his dernier resort; would it not be an injury of the highest degree, to prevent the exercise of his claim? Or, can any benefit arise to a community in general, when a part of that community exempts the remainder from the ultimate acquisition of its property? In a trading country, especially, the shortest methods that can be procured, should be allowed to creditors to acquire their just debts; and to deprive a subject of such means, is equally an hardship to him, and an injury to the country he lives in. How easy might it be for a bad man to mortgage his estate for its value, make sacred his person by privilege, and ruin his junior creditors: and how can it be said that the course of justice will not be affected; when a man who ought legally to be a prisoner, and his goods and chattels forfeited to his creditors, shall be turned
loose,

loose, whenever an assembly is to meet, and for so long as they may set, attended with equipage and servants; and, of the latter, most likely, as many as he pleases to take; and which, no doubt, he may take that occasion to convey where he pleases: and yet, all the time, he may be a freeholder, by lands intailed, or by right of marriage, or by the courtesy of England. However disinterested, however just, however worthy, the present representatives of Barbados are, and these undoubtedly have too much justice to make an ill use of any power; yet the time may come, when this may not be the case; and when the pernicious tendency of this privilege will be perceived; and when it will be found ultimately to be hurtful to the subject. The only plausible reason given in support of this privilege, is security to the constituents of their representatives services: now,

we find that the Barbadians have never wanted as able and honest representatives, as their country or any colony could afford, for near a century and a half; and they have never perceived, that they ever stood in need of a grant of privileges. A learned and ingenious member [u] (in whose abilities his country places great confidence, and from whose services his fellow-subjects form great hopes and expectations) seems to have had an eye towards the inconveniencies attending upon the exorbitant use of this privilege; when, at a meeting of the assembly of Barbados, on June 3, 1767, he moved, " that it
" should be declared, to be the sense of
" the house, that the exemption from ar-
" rests, and other disturbances of their
" persons and servants, was not intended
" by them to be construed, farther than

[u] Henry Beckles esq.

" was necessary to secure the personal
" attendance of each member on the
" house; and in no wise to interrupt the
" course of justice, which might affect
" them upon other occasions." This motion was unanimously approved.

As to the exercise of this privilege, as a security against arbitrary power, far be it from us to object to so useful a precaution; and could thus much of this privilege be obtained, unclogged with other circumstances, it undoubtedly would have its advantages. Every branch of legislature should be prevented from interfering with, or acquiring an undue influence over, each other: but care should be taken, that along with the corn, tares do not grow also. To the commons of England, there was a necessity for the exertion of this privilege, to protect them from the violence of former arbitrary reigns:

reigns: but sicce the Revolution, that happy æra, when liberty was secured by law, this necessity wears not so pressing an appearance; much less, when the royal power is delegated (and controuled by instructions) to a governor of a colony [x].

[x] So necessary was this privilege formerly, and yet so little stand could it make against violence, that in Henry the Eighth's reign, when the commons made a difficulty of granting the required supply, he sent for Montague, one of the members, who had a considerable influence on the house, and said to him, "Ho! man! will they not suffer "my bill to pass?" and laying his hand upon Montague's head, added, "Get my bill passed "by to-morrow, or else to-morrow this head of "yours shall be off". The next day the bill was passed. See Hume's History of England.—But will any man say, that the times now are not widely different? thank God, they are; and 'tis every man's business to enjoy the blessing without repining, or grasping at more.

Much

Much more indeed might be said upon this subject; but what however would with more propriety adorn the speech of a legislator, than grace the pen of an historian; who has already exceeded the limits he prescribed to himself. What has already been, or may farther be said on this subject, is offered with all imaginable respect and deference, to the present, honest and upright assembly of Barbados, who can have no interest divided from that of their country. The privilege of speech to the representatives of a people is a constitutional privilege, inherent in that body: it is strange then, that a gentleman of the speaker's lively imagination should appear not to know he possessed this valuable privilege, by making a demand of it. As to access to the King's representative, this privilege is in itself of so innocent and harmless a nature to the public,

public, that no more prejudice could arise from refusing its admission, than good could accrue by granting of it.

To conclude. These sallies of the speaker's genius bring to our remembrance a saying of King James the First, as related by lord Bacon: " When cardinal " Evereux (says Bacon) having in a sub- " ject of divinity sprinkled many orna- " ments of learning, the king said, they " were like the blue, and yellow, and red " flowers in corn, which make a pleasant " shew, but hurt the corn."

On the 1st of September 1767, at a meeting of the general assembly, a committee of that house was appointed to prepare a petition (in conjunction with a committee of the council) to be presented to the commons house of parliament of Great Britain, representing the distresses of

the

the island by the two last dreadful fires in the chief town, the intention of the inhabitants to rebuild the town on a safer plan, and to make convenient wharfs, and cleanse the Mole-head; and further representing the great expence attending these works, and the inability of the country wholly to provide for them: and therefore praying the assistance of that honourable house on the occasion. This is a representation just and necessary, and this a conduct much to the honour of the legislature of Barbados: no doubt, the reception that this petition will gain from the commons of Great Britain, will reflect equal honour upon that respectable body. The cleansing of the Mole-head, and erecting proper wharfs for the convenience of trade, are works of the utmost advantage, and therefore of the greatest consequence to this trading island; but whose utility will not be confined to this spot alone,

alone, but muſt ſpread its influence throughout all the Britiſh dominions. The Mole [y], when effectually cleaned, will again afford a ſafe retreat to ſhips of burden in the moſt tempeſtuous ſeaſon; whereas now it cannot protect the ſmalleſt veſſel: add to this, the alarming and increaſing inconvenience of landing and ſhipping all kinds of merchandize.

His majeſty having been pleaſed to appoint William Spry, eſq. governor of Barbados, that gentleman landed at Bridge-Town the 11th of February 1768; and was received with all the honours due to his ſtation. On the 18th the aſſembly attended the governor in council; when he made a ſpeech to both houſes: and on

[y] The Mole runs through the ſouth eaſt part of Bridge-town, and falls into Carliſle-bay: and is now choaked up by ſand and mud brought into it by the tides.

the same day the house of representatives resolved to settle three thousand pounds *per annum* upon the governor, and a bill to that effect passed the house; this bill passed the council also the 22d of March; when the speaker, accompanied by the whole house, waited upon the governor in council; and, in delivering the bill to him for his assent, the speaker addressed him in the following terms:

"May it please your excellency!

"By command of the house of as-
"sembly, and with the voice of unani-
"mity and concord, I have the honour
"to present your excellency with a
"faithful earnest of the general esteem.
"By this bill a large additional provi-
"sion, additional to that which is ap-
"pointed you by the crown, is here pre-
"sented you by the people, the better
"to enable your excellency to support
"the

" the dignity of your station, and give
" lustre to your authority: a tribute not
" more free, than founded in the most
" laudable desires, which, establishing
" your excellency's state in ease and inde-
" pendence, leaves you without a care, but
" for the public interest, and its honour.
" The time indeed has been, I should
" have rather said, the time has always
" been, when this tribute has been grant-
" ed in far happier circumstances of our
" country; but at no time was ever one
" resolved upon with a more perfect cor-
" diality, because at no time suggested
" by a more disinterested principle than
" the present. From hence your excel-
" lency will naturally suppose, that the
" circumstances of our country, suffer-
" ing under the pressure of repeated ca-
" lamities, could not fail to make a part,
" a serious part, of our consideration
" upon this interesting subject: yet, in

" settling

" settling a provision necessary for your
" excellency's honour, and our own, the
" assembly soon found it in their hearts,
" to give you the fullest pledge of their
" affection, rather than, with so many
" engaging motives to that affection,
" seem deficient in their accustomed be-
" nevolence; determining to invite your
" excellency to partake with us in the
" resources for our comfort, rather than,
" by a less generous proceeding, to in-
" volve you in a share in our misfortunes.
" Such, Sir, was the agreeable result of
" our unbiassed deliberations; and may
" your excellency's enjoyment of the fruits
" of them, be as pure and lasting, as the
" motive of our conduct in the gift
" was liberal and honest. The bill in
" my hand is intitled, 'An Act to raise
" a sum of money yearly to defray the
" expences of the government;' to which
" it is my duty to desire your excellen-
" cy's

" cy's aſſent, and my hope, that it may
" alſo meet with your entire approbation."

To this the governor gave the following anſwer:

" Mr. ſpeaker, and gentlemen!
" I return you my ſincere thanks for
" your very affectionate addreſs. I have
" the higheſt ſatisfaction in receiving
" your early, and cordial aſſurances, of
" concurring with me effectually in every
" meaſure, that can tend to promote the
" happineſs of this colony, as that will
" ever be the principal object of my
" wiſhes and labours. The generous at-
" tention you have been pleaſed to pay to
" my eaſe and welfare, demands the moſt
" grateful returns, and cannot but per-
" fectly anſwer the gracious intention of
" his majeſty, by leaving me without a
" care, but for his majeſty's honour, and
" the proſperity of this iſland."

In

In July a bill passed to raise a sum of money (upwards of two thousand pounds) for the repairs of Pilgrim-house. The Barbadians promise themselves much satisfaction under the government [z] of Mr. Spry; from whose good sense, and amiable disposition, they may reasonably expect a just administration; when the ease of the subject, and the dignity of the crown will be equally preserved; when the stream of government favour will flow through a clear and transparent channel; and when unanimity, so essential to the safety and happiness of every com-

---

[z] The present members of his majesty's council of Barbados are.

Sir John Gibbons, Bart. and K. B.

Samuel Rous,	Conrade Adams,	
John Dottin,	Gedney Clarke,	
Edward Jordan, } Esqrs.	Francis Ford, } Esqrs.
Henry Thornhill,	Rob. Braithwaite,	
Abr. Cumberbatch,	Irenæus Moe,	
Henry Frere,		

munity,

munity, will be promoted, and encouraged, under the auspicious influence of a mild, and able governor.

The present members of the assembly of Barbados:

Parish	Members	
S. Mich. Parish	Samson Wood, Patrick Lynch,	Esqrs.
Christ Church	Thomas Ince, Henry Beckles,	Esqrs.
S. Philip's	John Gittens, Thomas Drake,	Esqrs.
S. George's	Samuel Sedgwick, Eyre Wallcot,	Esqrs.
S. John's	Richard Downes, Benjamin Mallony,	Esqrs.
S. Joseph's	Henry Holder, Benjamin Mellowes,	Esqrs.
S. Andrew's	John Gay Alleyne, James Maycock,	Esqrs.
S. Thomas's	William Alleyne, George Sanders,	Esqrs.
S. James's	John Ridgway, Thomas Alleyne,	Esqrs.
S. Peter's	John Denny, Joseph Leacock,	Esqrs.
S. Lucy's	Hillary Rowe, Hillary Rowe junior,	Esqrs.

Of its Constitution.

THE government of Barbados consists of a governor, who is appointed by the king; a council of twelve men, who are also appointed by his majesty, by letters of mandamus; and an assembly of twenty-two freeholders, chosen by a majority of freeholders, from the several parishes. Two representatives are returned from each parish. The governor is the representative of the crown; he is commander in chief, chancellor, ordinary, and vice admiral of the island. The members of council (as privy counsellors) advise and assist the governor, in all matters relative to the government; and are a curb upon him, if he exceeds the bounds of his commission: they (as part of the legislature) form the upper house, and in passing all laws, act as the house of peers in Great Britain: the council board is wisely adapted as a balance in the legislative authority; it may always be a check upon an assembly, and a restraint upon a governor. The governor, and the members of council, constitute the courts of chancery and errors, where each member gives his opinion in all causes. The governor, as chancellor, grants administrations, and executorships of estates of persons dying intestate, to whom he pleases: he also admits licentiates, and grants probates to wills; he hath power to appoint and displace all military officers, and to dissolve the assembly, and also to place a negative upon all bills: judges of the courts, and justices of the peace cannot be appointed, but by and with the consent of the council, whose approbation or concurrence must be obtained when a judge is removed from his office. No member of council can be removed by a governor, without the

consent

consent of the majority of the council, unless on some very extraordinary occasion not fit to be divulged to the whole body. In such a case, the reasons for such suspension (or removal) are immediately to be transmitted to the king in council, where the member suspended may make his defence. A member of council vacates his seat, by absenting himself seven years from the council-board, without leave of absence obtained from the king, or from the commander in chief of the island. If there are less than seven members of council resident upon the island, the commander in chief hath power to fill up to that number, until his majesty's pleasure is known, that the business of the island may not be retarded[a].

[a] The members of council, while resident in the island, by virtue of their commission, are stiled Honourable, and precede Baronets. Custom too has given the title of his Excellency to the governor

governor always sits in council, even when acts are passed; a practice that seems to have been established by custom only; for it appears to be unconstitutional. It is not a custom adopted by all the colonies. The governor, besides his salary of two thousand pounds sterling, payable out of the four and half *per cent.* is intitled to a third of seizures; but he is restrained from receiving any present from the assembly, unless as a settlement made by the first assembly he meets after his arrival. This settlement has latterly been three thousand pounds *per annum* currency. In the absence of a governor, the senior member of council acts as commander in chief; but he cannot dissolve an assembly: nor can he remove or suspend any officer, civil or military, without the consent of seven members of council. In other respects he has the same power as a governor.

The

The president is allowed one half of the salary and emoluments allotted to the governor. Five members of council make a quorum to transact business, and to constitute a court of chancery, and court of error. The commander in chief collates rectors to the parishes of the island, which are eleven. The rectors perquisites are considerable; their income established by law is one hundred and fifty pounds *per annum*, exclusive of all presents, and other benefits. The clergy are all of the church of England. The representatives of the people are chosen annually, by virtue of a writ (or commission) issued by the governor in council, directed to the eldest member of council in each parish, authorizing him to convene the freeholders, and to receive their votes: afterwards, a return of the writ, with a certificate of the choice of the freeholders, is made to the governor in council, when the representatives take the state oaths, and oaths of office, before the governor and council; which they also do upon the accession of a new governor or president. The assembly chuse their speaker, who cannot act as such before he is presented to, and approved by the commander in chief. The speaker and eleven other members constitute a house for transacting of business. They chuse a clerk and marshal of their house. They may expel any of their members, and may give leave to two of them together to go off the island for six months for recovery of health. They have power to try and determine all controverted elections, and can adjourn themselves from day to day; all longer adjournments are made by the commander in chief, or with his leave. They, together with the governor and council, annually nominate the agent, the treasurer, the store-keeper of the magazines,

the

the comptroller of the excise, the gaugers of casks, and an inspector of health. Disagreements [b] have formerly arisen be-

[b] About the year 1728 a dispute arose between the council and assembly concerning the method of issuing orders for the public money; the former insisted upon that which was established by the king's instructions to the governor, the latter had discovered, as they thought, a method more beneficial to the country, by making a previous application to themselves necessary. Accordingly they framed an excise-bill in pursuance of this scheme: this bill the council rejected, and gave their reasons for their conduct. these reasons were drawn up by a committee, and were sent, together with a draught of the bill, to the secretary of state. The conduct of the council was approved, and an order was sent to the governor to reject the draught of the excise-bill, as contrary to the constant usage of Barbados, &c. Again, in president Berwick's time, the same topick was started, with some others equally prejudicial to the authority of the governor and council, and the like stagnation was given to public business. but the conduct of the council was again approved, and that of the assembly censured.

tween the council and assembly concerning the nomination of these officers, and also concerning the method of issuing the public money from the treasury; their disputes have gone so far, that references have been made to the throne. The offices of treasurer, and store-keeper, are confined to the members of the assembly. In passing all laws, the house of assembly forms that part of their constitution, which the commons house does in England. Four of the council nominated by the governor, and six of the assembly named by the speaker, are a committee for settling the public accounts of the island; among which number is the treasurer's account. The treasurer cannot pay any public money, nor make any particular appropriation of money, without an act of the island, or an order from the governor and council. Three of the council and four of the assembly

sembly are appointed a committee to correspond with the agent in Great Britain. The court of exchequer is held by a chief baron, and four assisting barons, appointed by the governor and council. Any three make a court.

Barbados [c] is divided into five precincts, though there are eleven parishes; a judge and four assistants preside in each precinct. They hold a court of common pleas for trial of all causes once every month, from the last Monday in January to the latter end of September. From

---

[c] St. Michael's precinct contains, St. Michael's, St. George's, and St. John's parishes.

St. James's precinct contains, S. James's and St. Thomas's parishes.

St. Peter's precinct contains, St. Peter's and St. Lucy's parishes.

Ostin's precinct contains, Christ Church and St Philip's parishes.

Scotland precinct contains, St. Andrew's and St. Joseph's parishes.

these

these courts appeals lie in all causes above ten pounds value to the governor and council: and from them in all causes above five hundred pounds to the king and council of Great Britain. The chief judges of the courts of common pleas take the probate of all deeds. The governor appoints the two masters in chancery, the escheator, and solicitor general. The attorney general is appointed by patent, the judge of the vice-admiralty court, the register, the clerk of the crown, the secretary, and clerk of the council, the provost marshal, and naval officer, are appointed by patent. The casual receiver and auditor general have their commissions from the crown, the surveyor general, and other officers of the customs, are appointed from the department of the treasury; and upon a vacancy in the customs the surveyor general nominates *pro tempore*. The justices of the peace are

appointed

appointed by a commission issued by the governor with the consent of the council; which commission is generally issued soon after the appointment of a governor. The governor, by and with the advice of the council, appoints a chief justice of the court of grand sessions, or general gaol delivery; which court is appointed by law to be held twice in every year. This court generally holds four days, and is formed by the chief justice, and any other five justices of the peace. Six freeholders from each parish are returned by the eldest member of council resident in each parish, by virtue of the governor's writ (or commission), to serve on the grand inquest, and petty juries. This court acquits or condemns all criminals,[a] the

[a] Governor Lowther once in the case of Brenan granted a pardon to the criminal before trial. A procedure unheard of in the constitution of Barbados, inconsistent, and unprecedented, however, the

commander

commander in chief having a right to respite those condemned for capital crimes from time to time: and to pardon those convicted of inferior crimes. The justices in their several parishes hold a quarter session for the appointment of constables, and rectifying of abuses. The governor appoints a coroner to each parish. Gunners and matrosses belonging to each of the five divisions are under the command of the colonels of foot to which each division belongs; but they are appointed by the commander in chief, at the recommendation of the said colonels. The commissioners for taking care of the fortifications are the members of council and assembly, and field officers belonging to each precinct. The governor, as captain general, usually presides at the coun-

culprit (whose crime was killing his antagonist in a duel) was wise enough to retire to England, and obtain a pardon from a higher power.

cils of war; but the commiffion of prefidet of the councils of war is often granted to the lieutenant general. There are fix regiments of foot militia in the ifland, and three of horfe, befides a troop called the horfe guards^e. There is an excellent armoury, and alfo a good train of artillery, in Barbados.

^e The method of lifting, raifing, and accoutring the militia, fee in the Laws of Barbados.

Of the Trade, Soil, and Climate.

NATURE hath been bountiful by fortifying the coast of Barbados, and rendering the greatest part of that island inaccessible to ships of fifty tons and upwards. An extensive reef of rocks runs from the south point easterly to the north-west. The other part of the coast the inhabitants have at a very great expence fortified, by erecting forts and batteries within gun-shot of each other; the repairs and maintenance of which amount to a great charge: an expence so heavy to the country, that it is to be hoped the government of Great-Britain will, some time or other, by their assistance, alleviate it.

The country abounds with plenty of provisions of all sorts, and the coast is well stored with a variety of good fish:

and in this country is preserved that antient British hospitality, for which Great Britain was once so deservedly famed.

It must not be concealed that this island, undoubtedly, wants an internal place of strength for the inhabitants, which would serve as a security, after an unsuccessful defence: such a fortification as might be erected, would, under pressing circumstances, be a means of preserving the island, until the king's fleet could get to its assistance.

The plantations of Barbados, oppressed by taxes, impoverished by mismanagement, and loaded by the great and necessary expences of their management (particularly, the advanced price of negroes), yield not now the profits they formerly afforded: notwithstanding the high

high estimation Europeans may set upon West India estates, yet it is an indisputable fact, that the landed interest of Barbados (that is throughout the whole island) does not clear *communibus annis* four *per cent.* estimating the principal at what land usually sells for: the destruction of the woods of that island, though it renders the country more healthful, hath decreased the quantity of rain, and hath been thereby detrimental to the planters [f]. The soil of Barbados is in

---

[f] To bear up against so many discouragements, the utmost skill ought to be exerted in adjusting the business of an estate, and, though it is true, that the want of seasonable weather is sufficient to baffle the greatest abilities of the planter, yet it is equally true, that the failure of these estates proceeds very frequently from unskilful management, so that when some estates, that are well attended to, yield a very profitable income, others again afford little or no profit. Indeed it may be said with justice and propriety, that an estate as often fails from the unskil-
general

general fruitful, but very different in different parts of the island, and frequently

fulness of the proprietor, in not maintaining a full quantity of stock upon it, as from the unskilfulness of the steward (or manager): for the former, however, some reasonable excuses may be made, as the want of credit (a circumstance always destructive to the good condition of a West-India estate) or the want of opportunity to purchase stock: but for the latter no just apology whatever can be offered. Thus, notwithstanding the uncertainty of profit, the unavoidable expence attending an estate is certain, and is inconceivably great. Suppose, for instance, an estate of only two hundred and sixty acres to work this properly, must be maintained upon it one hundred and eighty negroes, one hundred horned cattle, twelve horses, forty sheep, three tenants (or militia men) suppose with three in each family, who support themselves from the profits of the ground allowed them: a steward (or manager) whose annual salary may be from one hundred to one hundred and fifty pounds: an under steward (or driver), a distiller, and two apprentices, whose salaries together may be forty-five pounds *per annum*: add to this, the salaries of a town agent in the same estate. Some spots afford a heavy clay soil, others a light sand; some a dark heavy, others a light red earth, some parts wet and swampy, others dry and gravelly: but the land, almost every where, for the production of sugar, requires rich manure; the preparation of which shews the skill of the planter, as some parts of the island require a light, others a heavy manure; and sometimes

and book-poster at fifteen or twenty pounds each; of an apothecary at thirty, or forty pounds *per annum*; of a farrier at fifteen or twenty; the commissions of an English agent at two and an half *per cent.* freight of sugars, taxes, duties, repairs of buildings, and many incidental expences nor must we forget the maintenance of the proprietor and his family, with eight or ten servants. From these particulars may be learnt the reasonableness of the above assertion, that the landed interest in general does not neat four *per cent.* annually. The land, though long worn, will, it is thought by many good planters, produce as much as ever it did, assisted by manure.

both

both in the same estate. The manufacture of sugar is ingenious as well as useful. It is attended with great labour and expence, and requires skill and industry to perfect it. It was brought to pretty good perfection so early as 1650; but tobacco was first planted here, which at that time turned to no good account. The inhabitants were taught the art of making sugar by the Dutch. The cane plant was first brought hither from Fernambucca in Brasil. The Barbadians rear all their horned cattle and sheep, but few horses are bred here: these are brought chiefly from the continent of America, and some few from England: the English horses are best adapted for the saddle; the American horses for hard labour.

The trade of Barbados is yet flourishing and considerable, notwithstanding the discouragements given to it by taxes, by duties, by the accession of the large island of Jamaica, by the conquest of Grenada, by the acquisition of the late neutral islands, by granting a free port to Dominique, by the distillation of spirits upon the continent of America, by the want of a proper standard or regulation of the value of gold throughout the West India islands; and lastly, by the clandestine trade, which the Dutch of St. Eustatia have formerly been famed for.

The annual internal expence of Barbados amounts to sixteen thousand pounds, besides the considerable duties paid to the mother country. Bridge-town [g], the metropolis of that island, before the two

[g] Bridge-town is now rebuilding with a becoming elegance and uniformity; some useful measures having been taken by the legislature for that purpose.

destructive

destructive fires in 1766, consisted of about fifteen hundred dwelling-houses and stores, chiefly built of brick and stone, and which were in general spacious, and elegantly decent: the rents of the houses amounted to about forty thousand pounds *per annum*. There are in that island three other towns of smaller note, called Ostin's, St. James's, and Speight's. There are few public buildings in Barbados. The town-hall where the council and assembly meet, and where the courts of justice are held, the governor's house and arsenal situated a mile from Bridge-town, and the churches, are all that can properly be so termed. The churches are spacious, handsome buildings; the pews and pulpits are of cedar: and all the ornaments as decent as any where in the British empire.

The great value of Barbados to Great-Britain is best known from its vast consumption

sumption of British and Irish manufactures and commodities: add to this, the wealth expended by, and the consumption of Barbadians who reside in England: nor must we forget the large amount of the king's customs arising from the produce of this colony. It is judged, according to an accurate calculation, that four hundred ships of one hundred and thirty tons and upwards are employed in the trade of this island: from hence a nursery and support of seamen. It is supposed too, that the value of the exports from Great Britain alone, imported into this island, in certificate goods, British produce, and manufactures, is about eighty thousand pounds *per annum*. The goods sent from Great Britain are chiefly woollen, linen, Manchester velvets, silk, iron, brass, copper, leather, laces for linen, hats, wigs, shoes, stockings, china, glass,

earthen

earthen wares, pictures, clocks, watches, jewels, plate, gold and silver lace, medicines, oats, peafe, beans, cheefe, bacon, starch, oatmeal, gunpowder, bricks, tiles, lead, paint, oil, coals, cordage, sugar, pots, and drips, hoops, pewter, soap, candles, snuff, cut tobacco, pipes, cards, refined sugar, wine, beer, ale, cyder, perry, spice, fruit, tea, pickles, guns, swords, pistols, walking canes, horses, mules, grind-stones, paving-stones, books, toys, stationary, cutlery, Birmingham, and haberdashery wares, coaches, chariots, chaises, all sorts of houshold-goods, &c. besides the supplies from Ireland, and the very considerable importations of timber, fish, &c. from the northern colonies; add to this, the trade to Madeira and the coast of Africa, from which last place the importation of negroes is very great: a trade that employs many ships belonging to Bristol, Liverpool, Lancaster, and Glasgow, as well as from London.

As to the exports of Barbados, sugar is its staple: the following is a computation taken from good authority, of what may have been the exports of Barbados *communibus annis* [h] for the last ten years:

20000 hhds. of sugar, 6000 hhds. of rum, 4670 bags and barrels of ginger, 600 bags of cotton, } Shipped to London, Bristol, Liverpool, Lancaster, Falmouth, Whitehaven, and most other parts of Great Britain, the rum is usually re-shipped to Ireland.

500 hhds. of sugar, 1650 of rum, 10 of molasses, } to Philadelphia.

580 hhds. of sugar, 2580 of rum, 22 of molasses, } to Virginia and Maryland.

[h] 2200 hhds of sugar, and 7000 of rum, are supposed to be consumed annually in the island. An hhd. of sugar weighs from twelve to sixteen hundred weight, an hhd of rum contains 100 gallons. The cotton trade has been much neglected; from a proper supply of cotton, the inhabitants might manufacture some parts of their apparel, and thus the lower sort of the people might be usefully employed.

700 hhds.

700 hhds. of sugar,
2020 of rum, } to New England.
50 of molasses,

100 hhds of sugar, } to New York and Jersey.
450 of rum,

260 hhds. of sugar, } to N. and S Carolina,
1050 of rum,

120 hhds. of sugar,
1500 of rum, } to Newfoundland.
20 of molasses,

40 hhds of sugar, } to Bermudas.
180 of rum,

From the above calculation, may be learnt the great utility of this colony alone to the mother country; not only by the supply of its manufactures, which prevents large sums of money from being carried out of England to purchase these commodities in foreign countries, but also by employing and supporting a very great number of seamen, artificers, and manufacturers, who are concerned in the several branches of trade dependent on the sugar islands. If then this small colony is so useful to Great Britain, as from hence

hence it appears to be, of how much more confequence muft all her colonies together be found? Surely of fo much benefit, as to be intitled always to her protection, encouragement, and affiftance. From their refources the colonies claim a fhare of the merit of having raifed Great Britain to be one of the firft kingdoms in Europe for power and opulence, as fhe is undoubtedly the firft country in the world for affording every convenience and bleffing of life.

The white inhabitants of Barbados are computed to be about twenty-two thoufand, and the flaves to be about seventy-two thoufand [i]: a large number to be

---

[i] A ftate of flavery naturally fills an European mind with ideas of pity and deteftation, and furnifhes a plaufible objection againft thofe countries that admit it. but when we confider (what really is the cafe) that the negro flaves are conftantly fupplied

maintained

maintained in so small an island. In St. John's parish, about ten or twelve miles from Bridge-town, is a college for the education of youth; and a very large estate, capable of clearing three thousand pounds *per annum* English (or Sterling) money,

with food, with cloaths, with houses, with apothecaries to inspect their health; all which create a large annual expence to their masters; that though they labour much, yet that they have their hours and sometimes days of recreation, we are excited to conclude their situation to be less miserable, than that of the poor inhabitants of many European countries: nor have the slaves that idea of liberty which European nations have; and which, if they possessed, would tend much to heighten their wretchedness; but their ignorance in a great measure alleviates their unhappiness, and adds to their content. They who chuse baptism are not denied it but neither baptism, nor a residence in Europe, is sufficient to shake off their state of slavery. Few of these poor wretches shew any disposition to hearken to the doctrine of Christianity. they are so fond of their own idolatry, that it would be impossible to convert them.

was left by Mr. Codrington to support this charitable inſtitution; from whence, under proper regulations, many advantages might be enjoyed by the inhabitants of that iſland. There are two ſtreams in Barbados called rivers, one in the eaſt, and the other in the ſouth weſt part of the iſland. In the center are ſeveral bituminous ſprings, ſome of which furniſh the green tar, of great uſe in many diſtempers, and often ſupplies the want of pitch and lamp oil.

Barbados abounds with wells of exceeding good water, and contains large reſervoirs of rain water: the woods having been deſtroyed, and the land converted into corn and cane fields, the iſland preſents to the eye the moſt beautiful appearance of ſpring, ſummer, and autumn: nor is there any place in the Weſt-Indies comparable to Barbados for the elegancies and

and conveniencies of life. The fruits (amongst which, the pine and orange are in very great perfection) are seldom or never out of season, and are by no means inferior to the European fruits[k].

The conveniencies of travelling in this country are few; for though every mansion affords an hospitable reception to the traveller, yet, with good materials, the public roads are very bad. It ought to be the policy of every country to have the means of travelling made agreeable, and to open an easy intercourse with different parts of the country; and the Barbadians neglect their own interest, as well as convenience, by neglecting their public roads. Turnpikes might be established here; if not in the country, yet they may in the town, and the avenues leading

---

[k] For their description, see Hughes's Natural History of Barbados.

to the town; and the annual sum of money now uselesly raised in each parish, for repairing the roads, might be collected by a different tax, and formed into a fund, under the direction of commissioners in each precinct, who, employing skilful, and laborious surveyors, might make good roads, and alter the face of this country to a great advantage. Many horned cattle and horses are now killed every year by the badness of the roads: hence one source of the expences of the planter's estates.

The climate, though warm, is by no means unhealthful. The heat is much alleviated by a constant cool sea-breeze. The glass (or thermometer) seldom exceeds 88; but it is as seldom lower than 72. This will appear moderate, compared to some parts of the continent of America, where the glass has reached 103. Regularity here, as in almost all countries,

countries, will preserve, and sometimes will give, good health. Europeans, when they first come to this island, are too neglectful of the necessary care required in a hot climate, and often feel the fatal effects of such inattention; but the natives enjoy good health, and frequently live to a very old age. There were living in this island a few yeare ago, within six miles of each other, five men, whose ages together exceeded four hundred years; and there lately died in this island, at the advanced age of one hundred and ten years, Mrs. Vaughan, a gentlewoman who had always resided upon the island. She had eight brothers and one sister, who all lived to see the youngest upwards of sixty years old, the longevity of its inhabitants proves the healthfulness of a country. Nor must the author of these sheets neglect to relate what has fallen within his own observations on this subject.

subject. He knew two gentlemen, whose extreme ill health would not permit them to live in England, the one on account of a rheumatic, the other on account of a gouty complaint, much relieved, and their health preserved, by exchanging the climate of England for that of Barbados. From hence let us be taught, not to judge too rashly of the inconveniencies of a warm climate. God made all countries to be inhabited; and probably he has bestowed some advantages upon those climates between the tropicks, which colder regions want.

A LIST of the Commanders in Chief of Barbados from its First Settlement.

Anno
1629 Colonel Henry Hawley appointed Governor
1641 Philip Bell, Esq. Lieutenant Governor
1650 Francis Lord Willoughby, ⎫
1652 Daniel Searle, Esq.   ⎬ Governors
1660 Thomas Modiford, Esq.   ⎭
1661 Humphrey Walrond, Esq. President
1663 Francis Lord Willoughby, ⎫
1667 William Lord Willoughby, ⎬ Governors
1674 Sir Jonathan Atkins, Knt.   ⎭
1680 Richard Dutton, Esq. Governor
1685 Edwin Stede, Lieutenant Governor
1690 James Kendal, Esq.   ⎫ Governors
1694 The Hon. James Russel,   ⎭
1696 Francis Bond, Esq. President
1698 The Hon. Ralph Grey, Governor
1701 John Farmer, Esq. President
1703 Sir Bevill Granvill, Knt.   ⎫
1707 Mitford Crow, Esq.   ⎬ Governors
1711 Robert Lowther, Esq.   ⎭
1714 William Sharpe, Esq. President
1715 Robert Lowther, Esq. Governor
1720 John Frere, Esq. President
1721 Samuel Cox, Esq. President

Anno
1722 Henry Worsley, Esq. Governor
1731 Samuel Berwick, Esq. } Presidents
1732 James Dottin, Esq }
1733 Lord Viscount Howe, Governor
1735 James Dottin, Esq. President
1739 Robert Byng, Esq Governor
1740 James Dottin, Esq President
1742 Sir Thomas Robinson, Bart. } Governors
1747 The Hon Henry Grenville, }
1753 Ralph Weekes, Esq. President
1756 Charles Pinfold, Esq. Governor
1766 Samuel Rous, Esq. President
1768 William Spry, Esq. Governor.

FINIS.

Lightning Source UK Ltd.
Milton Keynes UK
UKOW07f1934210517
301695UK00008B/257/P